SO-BKT-338

Early To Learn

Early To Learn

JOY M. CRANDALL

DODD, MEAD & COMPANY · NEW YORK

ISBN: 0-396-06920-7
Library of Congress Catalog Card Number: 73-19088
Printed in the United States of America

To George and Winifred Harris and Hazel
Small Martin, three seniors whose 222 years
of experience helped me set up a harmoni-
ous school for the very young

Acknowledgments

It has been heartening to have a manuscript generate so much interest, and the encouragement of many whom I admire in the field has helped the growth of this book. Special appreciation for thoroughly studying the original material is expressed to Dr. Edith Dowley, head of the combined demonstration Nursery Schools at Stanford University; Dr. Joseph Havens, of Amherst College, Quaker psychotherapist, educator, and writer; and Dr. Katharine Whiteside Taylor, mother of the cooperative nursery school movement.

The exciting adventure of recording the integrity of conscientious schools would not have been undertaken without the inspiration and practical prodding of Patricia Prins Hamill, Chester A. Koehler, and Marilyn Haley Trimble, each a real professional in his or her special field.

Dr. Stanley Coopersmith, John Otto, Willa Chapman Quillen, Libby Byers, and Dr. Millie Almy also cheered me over some hurdles.

Then, Frances Taliaferro, an editor, took the manuscript under her wing as a whole, rather than in parts, and went even further by editing her heart into the final book.

Most of all, to the families for allowing these memorable candid views of their school children to be published and to the photographers I wish to say thank you. The world will delight in your children.

JOY M. CRANDALL

Foreword

It is a pleasure to recommend *Early To Learn* to parents, teachers and all others interested in guiding the development of young children. The psychological and educational principles set forth are sound and good. The great value of the folio, however, lies in the excellent way each need and procedure is illustrated. These photographs are so well selected and adapted to the principles being set forth that their meaning is abundantly clear. Since studies indicate we remember twice as much of what we see as what we hear, this collection of pictures makes learning both easy to absorb and to remember. One feels throughout Mrs. Crandall's great sensitivity to the needs of children and the adults who guide them, developed through her own rich experiences as teacher and mother. It will be a valuable addition to libraries both in schools and homes concerned with releasing the full potentials of young children.

KATHARINE WHITESIDE TAYLOR

These schools and educational groups generously opened their doors to candid photography:

American Indian Division, U. F. G. M. C.
Bel-Aire Nursery School, Inc. and Bel-Aire Kindergarten
Bing Nursery School, Stanford University
Children's Learning Center, Behavior Therapy Institute
Cottage Parent Cooperative School
Creative Nursery School of Jeanette Parfitt
Diablo Valley Montessori School
Ding-Dong-Belle Nursery School
F. Y. T. Schools, Inc. (Formative Years Teaching)
Guide Dogs for the Blind, Inc.
Iolani School
Janus School
Johrei Summer Camp
Junior School
Luther Burbank Children's Center
Marin Friends Meeting

Merrie•Go•Round School & "One O'Clock Scholars"
Miss Kate's Classical Music Kindergarten Hour
Miss Kate's ABC Hour for Preschoolers
Montessori School of Yvonne van Boeckel
Nature Conservancy, Inc., Camp Unity II
Phoebe A. Hearst Preschool Learning Center of the
    Golden Gate Kindergarten Assoc.
R. L. D. S. Vacation School
Redwood High School Child Development Classes
St. Vincent Daycare Nursery
St. Vincent School
Tamalpais Valley Kindergarten
Twin Cities Parent Participating Nursery School
University of Southern California Preschool
Y. W. C. A. Preschool Dance Program

Contents

Let each become all that he was created
capable of being: expand, if possible, to his
full growth; and show himself at length in
his own shape and stature, be these what
they may.

THOMAS CARLYLE

Introduction

The essential precept of good education is that it is a joy to learn. This book attempts graphically to demonstrate that joy, and to provide inspiration and practical help to those dealing with early learners. I am thinking particularly of prospective teachers and aides in the Nursery–Kindergarten field, who have often encountered in their teacher training the anesthetic effects of too much lecturing and too many heavy textbooks. In working with preschoolers one is especially aware of the inadequacy of words to communicate the child's response to life. The candid pictures in this book, gathered in various schools over a period of years, attempt to record what the children themselves have to teach. Teachers immersed in the language of pedagogical textbooks tend to forget that young children do not speak textbookese. In fact, they often speak very little, and the non-verbal communication of these photographs is what many teachers need.

Early To Learn should also be of value to young families who are enrolled in cooperative nurseries, or who are considering starting their own schools. Good schools by no means all sing the same tune, but they do harmonize with the best interests of the children and families they serve. And just as teachers can learn from students, schools can learn from each other. I have, for instance, included pictures from two schools for special students. We can all benefit from some of the discoveries made by innovative teachers of the mentally retarded, the emotionally disturbed, or the gifted.

So many avenues are being explored in education that discussions of methods sometimes overshadow goals. We want to guide young children to blossom in each other's presence, and equip them to find their own way to the joy of learning. Dr. Esther P. Edwards counsels, "Let's be grateful for every addition to the techniques and tools which we can use to help children. Let us try to find out how best to employ each approach: when, with whom, for what reason, under what circumstances." It is the aim of this book to offer practical suggestions to meet the child's needs.

Good nursery schools range all the way from lavish model institutions to temporary arrangements to simple home situations. What they have in common is an atmosphere that children find both comfortable and stimulating. Sometimes children spend the first weeks at school wanting to explore the equipment and investigate the child-sized world before they go on to relate to teachers or other children. In a comfortable environment planned to nursery scale, the child first strengthens his feeling that he is a whole, normal, and belonging person. If the staff has chosen supplies with care and ingenuity, the child will then be drawn into the imaginative exploration of his surroundings.

When I called at a slick-looking new nursery school in an exclusive neighborhood, I found locked doors and an aloof teacher. The children had obviously been herded into the yard so that the rooms wouldn't become disarranged, and each door and room was kept secured unless it was actually being used. The restrictive climate and dozen cowed students could not compare to a happy, "live" situation, no matter how glamorous the physical plant.

Katharine Whiteside Taylor's books have enlightening chapters on new schools and how to start them. She points out that the prime problem is finding a usable building and getting through local planning and licensing agencies. Once established, a good school eventually combines the best atmosphere and adequate supplies. The schools in this book have been established long enough to have gradually acquired what they need. They demonstrate that openness and beauty may abide in the most unpretentious, obscure, or unlikely building.

It would be presumptuous if not impossible to prescribe a perfect teacher for the very young. The qualities desirable for all skillful teaching are essential here. Perhaps it's fairer to say that a school might hope to find, in the combined talents of its staff, the best teaching habits and the most agreeable personality traits. The following examples speak for themselves.

On a rainy February day a large package of nursery school supplies arrived and I took seven children into the kitchen area to help open it. Two children requested new items from the package, three chose the empty box to use, one wanted the colorful twine for a collage, and four-and-a-half-year-old Ricky asked for the wrapping paper. Ricky showed the paper to the teacher with whom he related best. On a low table in her room were displayed some of her collection of U. S. Presidential pictures. After studying the stamps on the wrapping paper with a magnifying glass, Ricky asked his teacher, "Is Washington on the one-cent stamp because he was the first President and Jefferson on the three-cent stamp because he was the third?" She was astounded and said that that was possible and she would check. On her coffee break she called a philatelic store and learned about the Presidential Stamp Series. For the next few weeks she gradually fed Ricky information until he was satisfied. Ricky had postulated a theory of his own from random facts and the teacher had done all she could to encourage his emerging inductive reasoning.

Cassandra, a teen-age aide giving directions for Indian sand painting, said simply, "Watch me paint freely with one tiny brushful of mucilage, and shake one handful of sand on my paper. Then you create on your own dark, stiff paper." A participating mother volunteer, working with another group, kept up a running commentary. "Don't you touch the glue, you might get sticky, and only use a little bit; don't take too much on the brush, and put it on quickly before it dries. No, no, don't get it in gobs like that; no, don't give the brush to Carl, give it to me to put back in the bottle. Now be careful about sand in your fingernails; it might get in your eyes. Here, let me hold your brown paper and shake it for you; now, you wash your hands right away. No, no, teacher will put your picture in your locker after it dries." She managed in one breath to cover most of the poor teaching techniques, only missing asking the child whether he was trying to make a man or a tree! Guess which group of children learned the most and made dramatic sand paintings over and over.

A new nursery school in a recreation district building had the serious problem of being unable to fence any of the property because of neighboring gardens. The staff and recreation district Board racked their brains, but could only conclude that for outside play the youngsters would occasionally be transported to a safe park. The first two weeks of school were rainy, so the small group of children launching the center were satisfied with the indoor equipment and space.

One of the teachers had an inspiration and called a "committee" meeting of the children to discuss the fact that when it stopped raining they would not be able to use the running space outside because of the adjacent gardens. She felt that they would understand better if they discussed it thoroughly. The children began making spontaneous suggestions: "One at a time could play outside with a teacher," "We could promise not to go near the rose gardens," "There could be a make-believe fence," "Chalk could mark where we could step." Alison said, "My granddaddy lived in the desert and he said he put prickly rope around his tent in a circle because snakes would not crawl over the prickles with their tender bellies. We could all be pretend snakes and lizards and tender things, and put a big rope and never go over it."

On the first sunny day they piled into the car and bought the thickest rope the teachers had been able to locate by phone. Each day the group helps set out the rope fence. As new children join the school, the "committee" explains its one important rule. The solution has been successful. Good teaching makes possible democratic procedures that would be unworkable in a dictatorial situation.

The final example is of a teacher's creative interaction with a parent, rather than with children or other staff members. In a preadmission interview a mother expressed her deep uneasiness at allowing four-year-old Greg to be anywhere without her personal supervision. She wanted to enroll him, but she hesitantly confessed her fears that he was a pyromaniac. She had caught him time after time hiding in a closet or under the house, playing with matches. "What if he sets the school on fire? I don't know which way to turn. I've punished him every way I know."

The teacher promised to give the matter thought. She called and asked the mother's permission to meet Greg at home and to bring a science experiment used with four-year-olds. She took the oxygen experiment, complete with three short candles in holders, sturdy matches, and one small, one medium, and one large jar. First she taught Greg the word "horizontal" and he practiced holding the match horizontally, then lighting the match, then lighting the candles. She discussed oxygen in relation to what Greg knew of plants' producing it, and pointed out that candles need oxygen as people do. She and Greg simultaneously placed the jars over the three candles. Greg was delighted to see the flames go out in order of the oxygen content of each jar. Four-year-olds normally repeat the experiment as long as they are allowed to do so, and Greg was no exception.

The teacher then suggested to the mother that if Greg could do the oxygen experiment carefully in the presence of adults, perhaps he could safely light a fire in the fireplace in his father's presence, or light candles for the supper table under his mother's supervision. The mother was readily converted to the constructive approach and carried it one step further by promising Greg her silver candle snuffer, an unused wedding gift, so he could also snuff candles each night. Greg did well in school with teaching that was not only preventive but creative, and the candle snuffer became his most prized possession.

Children's lives are in many ways narrower today than ever before. They may have viewed moon-walks on television, but their own experience of people is often limited to a small range of ages and occupations. Many children know only their own generation and that of their parents. If they live in a neighborhood of young families, they are unaware of old people, and they may see far-away grandparents very seldom. Children living with divorced mothers often feel the lack of a man in their lives. Even if parents are happily married, fathers usually spend most of the child's waking hours away from home, and business trips or long commutes prolong the father's absence.

If a school can provide contact with both men and women, young and old, the child's experience is immeasurably enriched. Many schools that want to improve their teacher–pupil ratio try to find volunteers or paid helpers; older people, if they are of the right disposition, are a wonderful addition. One school hires a pleasant elderly woman as part-time secretary, extra lap, hand-washer, and hugger. She also has time to chat reassuringly with parents during the difficult fifteen minutes at the end of school, when teachers are busy getting children and their equipment ready for home. One of the happiest experiments at my school was finding a retired gentleman who came to be a "grandfather aide." The children had a very special feeling about him. A magic bond quickly springs up between the old and the very young; children who could scarcely speak, proudly proclaimed "Grandfather Harris" as their own. Many children confided to me that although the grandfather worked with all the pupils, "he likes me the most" or "I'm his special child." In older people who are temperamentally suited to work with children, there seems always to be enough affection to go around.

A practical advantage of hiring retired people is that their salaries must be low so that they can keep their Social Security benefits. This means that the teacher–pupil ratio can be adjusted beneficially, without undue expense to the school. Another practical point is that a "grandfather aide" with an interest in, say, carpentry may help the children when regular teachers do not have time for individual supervision at the workbench. The "grandfather aide" may also take an interest in fix-it jobs around the school!

"Grandmother aides" are just as needed and just as helpful as grandfathers. One grandmother had moved to our town from a distant place and was lonesome. She made herself a long red velvet dress and each December she goes from school to school as "Mrs. Santa," chatting with children. (Many youngsters who fear Santa's long white beard are not afraid of her.) Sometimes I took groups of children to a home for active retired people. The children sang for them; the older people sewed stuffed toys for the school as a thank-you. Senior Citizen Clubs can be encouraged to put preschool visits on their lists of activities.

For instance, an elderly woman who knew all about birds came to talk to the children. I paid her a "transportation fee" because it made her feel an essential part of the school to be part of the budget. Some sort of financial involvement for aides is important. (In the same way, I never gave a whole scholarship, but always half ones. If the family paid half, they felt more involved in the school.)

"Resource people" of all ages who come to share the things they love can be an important part of the life of the school. Naturalists who love the area they live in; the "ice cream lady" who helps the children make their own dessert; a Chinese father who tells about Chinese calligraphy—all have much to give. Amateurs who are eager to share and to learn are the most welcome. A steady diet of experts turns children off; they can't compete. I love music but am no musician; the children "catch" music from me, with the feeling that *anyone* can enjoy and pursue it.

In seeking a school for three- to five-year-olds, parents naturally try to find one in which they and their children feel comfortable. General questions such as "What is your educational philosophy?" are answered by brochures and by observation. Specific questions such as "How do you handle the holidays?" can also help families find an educational home.

Three schools I've observed have entirely different approaches to Christmas. The first has a full-blown celebration. Weeks are spent preparing Christmas ornaments, decorations, and presents. All crafts, music, stories, and excursions are centered on the gift-giving spirit. A local fireman comes to school dressed as Santa and the children put on a play, acting Santa, reindeer, or angel parts. The child's entire family attends the Christmas party and gifts are exchanged all around. The excitement runs high and the families are proud of all the participation. The philosophy is that it may be exhausting, but it comes only once a year.

A second school believes holidays should be exclusively home-centered, and it avoids anything unusual in its routine on the theory that children are over-stimulated by group festivities. The school purposely has its parent get-together late in January, avoiding any theme except demonstrations by the staff of the children's science, art, carpentry, and language projects. Copies of the children's favorite music are distributed, and questions about school procedure are answered. "We take care not to believe everything your child says about home, and we hope you do not believe all he tells you about us" is the usual opener.

The third school steers a holiday course in between the two extremes. Along with its regular projects, it decorates simple candles suitable for Christmas or Chanukah. The children learn about bells of many lands and special holiday foods from various nations. One year a piñata may appear in the entry, and another year, decorated wooden shoes. "Mrs. Santa" comes for an informal visit, and any child who wishes may give her messages for her husband, or give her a used toy for Santa (the local veterans' group) to repair for the needy.

All three schools are well-run and are solidly supported by their parent bodies. As with everything from friendship to autos, different schools suit different people, and it is wise to investigate before enrolling yourself and your child. Just as the needs of the child vary according to individuality and timing, the needs of each family are unique. For example, a helter-skelter family may need a well-organized school that helps provide a little sense of order.

One young mother seemed verging on a nervous breakdown; her little Ruthie and Davey were nervous wrecks, too. When the mother told Mrs. T. that she was at the end of her rope, Mrs. T. asked her to describe an average day. It turned out that the mother kept an immaculate kosher household, including different sets of dishes. After her recent hysterectomy she had resumed all her normal routines before feeling strong. Her elderly and demanding aunt was with them. Her husband travelled often so she did double duty, as single parents are forced to do. She had other worries and felt exhausted all the time.

Mrs. T. asked the mother why she expected so much of herself. For one week, could she possibly nap during the three hours Ruthie and Davey were at school? Further, could she let the fussy aunt do some of the exacting chores, and she herself get a rocking chair in which to spend time relaxing with the children? (At school, Ruthie and Davey had demonstrated an insatiable desire for lap-sitting.) The young mother was so weakened that she agreed.

Often families can't change damaging patterns without professional guidance, but this mother's will power was at a low ebb. After a few remonstrances about how guilty she would feel just to rest and play with her children, she gave in easily. Her physical recuperation from self-enforced pressures helped her gain a better perspective and find the energy for a sensible schedule. And Ruthie and Davey benefited even more.

Since families differ so, the best advice is "*Don't* take people's advice; rely on your own instincts with your own child." If one helpful piece of advice had to be given, it might be "Speak softly and slowly and face-to-face with your preschooler." That would avoid a number of common pitfalls: the child's having to converse eye-to-kneecap, the mother's shouting from room to room or kitchen to yard, hasty orders, noise, and inevitable confusion.

Speaking face-to-face gives each child a moment of individual attention. Children, including twins, do not react at all in the same way to the same situations. Julie, who thinks about her actions in advance (and who is often mislabelled stubborn), may need to be told quietly, "In ten minutes when the kitchen timer rings, please wash your hands and come to lunch. You may help me wash dishes later." Tommy, a more instant child who does not enjoy thinking things out beforehand, will react best to "I'll wash your hands so you can put napkins on the table now." A third child, pliable Donna, may always be under foot "helping" every step of the way. Endless patience with Donna is easy to advise but difficult to practice.

In conclusion, from the vantage point of having raised three children who luckily matured nicely, I can say that there is no easy way to be a parent. A parent is unrealistically supposed to be some sort of emotional and physical savings bank from which withdrawals may be freely taken. It's harder to arrange for deposits. One answer is to let the children have the companionship of a good school as soon as possible. If no school suits you, start a cooperative school with the aid of other families and some good books such as those listed in the Bibliography.

In many cases, as in mine, academic familiarity with children and a dusty degree in Education may not make it immediately clear that one does not "teach" a child anything. One makes arrangements whereby a child wants to teach himself. One quietly sets examples. A child learns to like learning, and we gradually acquire enough wisdom to avoid putting unnecessary obstacles in his way.

A CHILD NEEDS

recognition and respect

love

security

enriching, ever-widening experiences

A CHILD THRIVES ON

friendships,

friendships,

friendships,

and more friendships

individual attention from teachers who care

a growing sense of humor

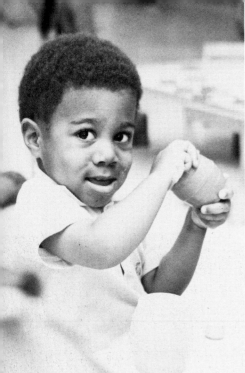

the ability eventually to laugh at an occasional failure of his own

the self-esteem that comes with frequent successes

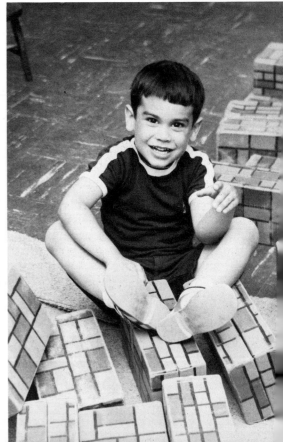

unhurried time to explore his interests

the joy of creating a larger image of himself through each new discovery

the feeling that he can control his own environment

freedom of action within sensible limits set by adults she can trust and respect

SCHOOL GIVES

a child plenty of opportunities to express and explore his own uniqueness

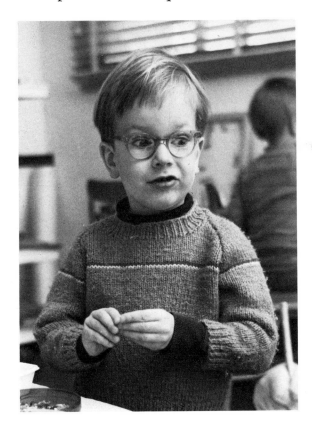

and freedom to work and play at his *own* rate, never "hurry, hurry." A healthy child is rarely lazy, but he may balk at the demands of an imposed schedule that squelches his interests and forces him to be what he isn't.

Some children are readier for school than others. Many bounce into school with open arms, like a three-year-old who invariably said every morning, "I'm here! You can start." But many feel ambivalent about leaving home.

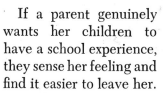

If a parent genuinely wants her children to have a school experience, they sense her feeling and find it easier to leave her.

Considerate schools think of orientations. Some have a morning before school starts when parents and children can explore the building together and learn something of schoolday routine. Others have staggered starting days so that children can come in smaller groups than usual. (This school has a "second story" playhouse area which makes the most of high ceilings.)

Loving parents are free with good-bye hugs and kisses, even extending them to extra children at times.

Security is found in many forms. Some children look for it in physical closeness to teachers or other grown-ups. This "grandfather aide" had no objection to being climbed over or sat on. Patient, undemanding grown-ups ease the way for cautious children.

At least one solid, wholesome relationship with an adult essentially precedes the ability to get along with contemporaries. At this age, too, proximity to an adult helps children want to learn.

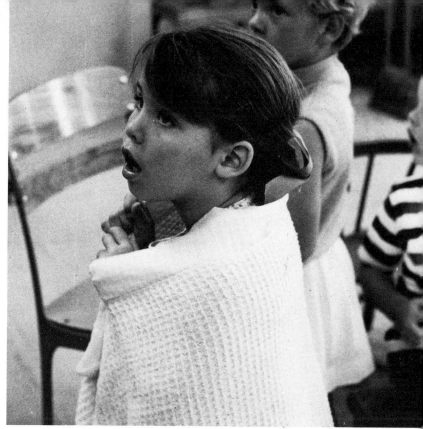

Some children may need the reassurance of a favorite toy or blanket in early days at school. Most teachers prefer to have personal treasures stay at home, but not if that will mean that the child rejects school. Children let go voluntarily as they become involved in interesting activities.

New experiences can be gently introduced. The twist board had just arrived at this school.

Shy children can be drawn into activities that they find inviting. The children are encouraged but not required to try everything; they are *invited* to join in. This group sat down with a box of drumsticks that the children had helped to make from broomsticks. The teacher drew large chalk circles on the floor to represent drums, and began to tell a story which the children accompanied. Sometimes they discovered a drumbeat they wanted to remember, and jotted it down in dots and dashes on huge papers hung on the wall—just like a real drum book from Africa that a mother happened to bring to school that day.

Children enjoy frequent successes which add to their self-esteem. These boys have recently acquired the finger dexterity to manipulate small pieces, and since children manipulate "things" before they manipulate "ideas," the staff encourages the immediate gratification that comes with satisfying their new ability.

A child learns to maintain her identity in a small group, later can manage independence within a large one. Children get nervous and emotionally overcharged in too big a group; they feel they have no control over the situation. What is "too big" depends on the child's maturity. A very mature two-year-old can hold his own in a group of three or four. A five-year-old can feel in charge of himself with as many as eight.

Children learn from experience that a few cooperating can enjoy and accomplish what one alone would find difficult.

They begin to develop helpful attitudes. She offers to pour water for one of his projects. (All sorts of unbreakable containers are used in sand and water play, but teachers caution children never to use a bottle at home without permission. A teacher's warning is usually more effective than a parent's, because teachers say "no" less often than parents do.)

But there are still times when children have mixed feelings about their work, about their teachers, and about cooperating with one another.

Sometimes it's best to leave children to deal with their own minor squabbles, which are often settled in a delightful way without adult interference.

When a teacher does intercede, she uses preventive, constructive and *private* discipline, sometimes picking up the child and removing him physically with a reassuring smile and no words. The wise teacher is aware that quarrels in school may be colored by conflicts that long pre-date school days.

Team teaching often enables one teacher to "float" and give individual attention where it seems called for. This kind of interest is especially good for the child who is so easy to work with in a group that he rarely gets special attention.

Children feel free to express themselves to adults they like and trust, especially as they learn in various ways that life is sometimes sad. This boy is grieving over the death of a school pet, both in words and in wholesome tears.

A child reaps untold rewards from contact with people of different generations and occupations. This mother is a newspaper editor who talked to the class about her work. Children are interested in what their parents do all day, and some schools require that parents share their professions either by visiting the class or by inviting small groups to their places of business.

Children who may not see their grandparents very often take special pleasure in stories read by a "grandfather aide."

Local colleges can be invited to send psychology major volunteers; this college student was doing an in-depth study of normal children.

The "ice cream lady" started as a volunteer and is now a regular visitor to schools in her neighborhood. She brings the freezer and the ingredients, and helps the children do each step themselves while she explains what is happening. Every community is full of people who love their work and who can communicate their pleasure to children.

Mrs. Terwilliger is a volunteer who tramps through the countryside on nature walks with preschoolers and their parents. Children may learn to distinguish hemlock by its smell or to "fly" like each different bird that passes. More than that, they absorb respect and love of nature from someone whose joy in it is contagious.

Little children look up to older ones. Teen-age volunteers are competent and imaginative; they benefit from the admiration of the younger ones. This school employs and trains Neighborhood Youth Corps boys. Adults often tend to "take over," but teen-agers seem to sense when to let little children do things for themselves (perhaps because they can still remember what it's like to be bossed by parents).

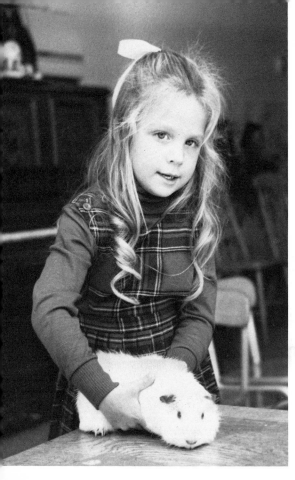

Gradually children can work up to familiarity with big animals. This boy is offering the St. Bernard a spoonful of water.

Children learn to take responsibility for live animals. This class has both tropical fish and a friendly toad to care for.

The more children can learn from animals, the better, especially soft ones that encourage gentle kindness. Families can share small, gentle pets that allay fears.

Children are enchanted to see plants and animals grow. They get a sense of nature's rhythms when they can plant a seed, water it, and watch its greening, and eventually pick and eat—a radish!

But it's hard to notice yourself growing, and adults seem so huge that children feel they'll never be that big. At times a child needs to feel taller than grown-ups, to feel bigger than his whole world.

The child's very being is hidden and revealed in his body and its movements. He is encouraged to get acquainted with his body's capabilities. Here the children do a "Good morning, feet, good morning, ankles" routine. One non-conformist puts his foot up instead of his hands down. Another sits silently through each dance session but insists on always attending.

Some children will sway to the music. The teacher sways and moves her arms, and soon everyone is moving. As the teacher suggests various animals and things that move gracefully and easily, the children begin to "be" those things: trees, clouds, snakes, kites. If the teacher has real balloons on hand, the children love to "help" the balloons move to the music.

Children are encouraged to tumble and do acrobatics in a safe place with a competent adult. An excursion to see a high school gymnastic team is a great inspiration to boys, who are generally not so limber as girls.

Balloon dancing is almost irresistible; even timid children use their bodies freely. A teacher and a small group of children listen to classical music in a quiet room.

Children enjoy soft, restful, slow songs pitched in their range, and musical finger-play games expand vocabulary. The teacher always faces the children, whether she plays the piano or leads finger-play songs like this. Then they can respond to her facial expressions and imitate her movements.

Children learn to listen and "be" the music. They have no more difficulty reading music than reading English. In this school, treble and bass clefs are painted on a large canvas. The teacher gives children notes on the pitch pipe and they quickly learn where middle C is. Then she plays one note higher and they literally step up on the scale. Soon they can follow a simple tune and dance it on the scale. What one learns with the *body*, one remembers.

Children take naturally to dramatic play. This girl is Little Miss Muffet; the group took turns acting the spider, the girl, the tuffet, the audience. The possibilities for dramatic play are unlimited: puppets, toy people in playhouses, newspaper hats, pantomimes. The senses and the emotions are exercised in wholesome acting out, creatively guided.

Parents and teachers should silently re-call that *action* speaks to the condition of the child and that wordiness shatters and confuses. A child often says "Watch me," rarely "Talk to me." As Laura Huxley says, "Words are good servants but bad masters."

Children learn more through their own experience than through being bombarded with words. This girl has made her own stilts out of two large empty juice cans with the ends in. Ropes are threaded through holes punched on each side of one end. When she holds the ropes taut and walks on the cans, she has a whole new feeling of size.

Through experiments that develop all five senses, children establish their relationship to the world. Here a child feels, smells, and tastes potatoes that the class has grown, cooked, and mashed.

Sometimes a child knows what she is touching and sometimes it is a guessing game. (The touching is more important, but the guessing fascinates her.) It might be play dough made by the children themselves, soap whipped in warm water, gelatin that didn't set, loose dry flour, wet wallpaper paste, gritty cornmeal, warm starch, grated carrot, shaving lather, soft noodles.

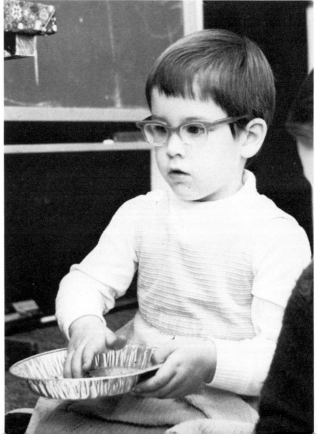

The same substance can offer very different tactile experiences.

The messiest craft projects are often the most engrossing.

Children are interested in and want to handle everyday items that adults take for granted, such as the flag.

The kindergarten way of tying shoes is to make the first simple knot, and then with two large loops repeat that same step.

Easy clothing, with no complicated or inaccessible fastenings, helps a child to take care of himself. This two-year-old has gone to the bathroom unaided. Though he may need assistance to get his clothes back in order, the important thing is that he did not need help to get his trousers down in time.

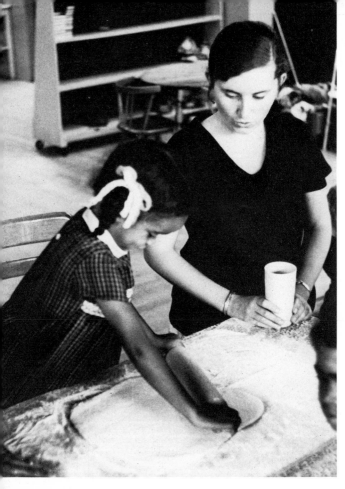

rolling pin and a plastic tumbler to cut biscuits which they sprinkle with cheese, bake, and enjoy immediately.

Wise schools serve nutritious snacks only. Non-foods are too readily available elsewhere. Children set the table, arrange flowers and place-marks, and enjoy attractively presented food. They love fresh and dried fruits, and many raw vegetables such as mushrooms and cauliflower are offered. They even nibble the lettuce brought for the class rabbit. Other good snacks are squares of cheese or cooked tongue, tiny rounds of luncheon meats, pitted olives, egg slices, yoghurt, spoonfuls of honey. Cookies can be cut out of a variety of breads, sprinkled with raw sugar, and baked a minute. Sometimes families bring special treats like smoked oysters, avocados, or clam chowder.

Children like to prepare snacks for the group. These boys and girls have made their dough from scratch after learning about each ingredient. They use a wooden

Children can learn to work carefully with real kitchen utensils. The safe side of this blunt-end knife is identified with a piece of colored tape.

This boy was mixing gelatin outdoors on a nice day. Other good projects are punch made of frozen juices; soup stock; pudding; milk drinks; pancakes. Pouring and measuring are fun, and cooking projects teach the importance of accurate measurements.

Some children have no experience with taking turns until they get to school. Table games provide a good opportunity. The immediate pleasure of receiving the lotto picture helps to teach children to raise their hands when their cards turn up. "Please pass the T for tea-kettle" gets the card and "Hey, me, me" doesn't. Sometimes the first child whose set is filled in gets to be the teacher for the rest of the game, and the child is even fussier about manners than the teacher was.

Children like to practice with volume and its relationship to quantity and to the shape of the container.

The teacher uses the oldest math during juice time and gives each child 1/3 cup + 1/3 cup + 1/3 cup because she knows they equal three times as much juice as one full cup spilled.

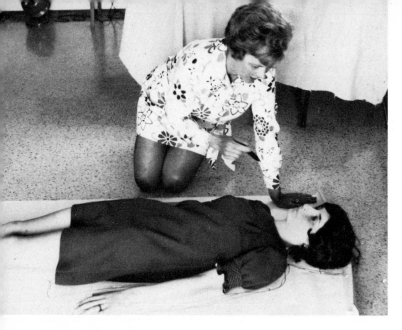

Thoughtful teachers always experiment with every detail of a future activity before scheduling it in the planning calendar. "No, the floor in this room is too cold to lie on, and the beams look as if they're descending on me. This would be a hard, cold, frightening experience. We'll have to find some place else to do the outlining of the children."

Careful but flexible planning brings rewards. The boy points with pride to the largeness of himself. His teacher found a pleasanter place to make his outline on brown paper. He has filled in his own shape and now it is mounted on a fence near the school entrance.

Confusion is as vexing to children as it is to adults. Teachers do well to give clear, well-thought-out directions. "One of you may divide the clay in half; the other one may take first choice."

There is no "ideal" curriculum. A teacher who cares about the children's emerging abilities and about the subject matter can use almost any approach or techniques effectively, if she is flexible enough to take advantage of natural opportunities. The children in this school helped raise the owl from a lost baby. He has been the subject of art work, of stories they've written, of science lessons, of songs. Wanting to learn about this particular owl led them to develop many other skills.

Excursions and field trips need thorough planning, with particular care for safety. This "mountain climbing rope" is used for crossing streets, entering museums, walking to local bulldozer sites or ice cream parlors. It is also used for fire drills. If safety procedures are a matter of routine, no one panics in an emergency. (Another good excursion routine is to carry litter bags on each outing, because children love to pick up trash.)

It is essential to learn the importance of obedience in matters of safety. One of the class fathers invited these children to visit the Guide Dog School, where they saw how guide dogs learn to obey.

A teacher does not assume that a child has learned the intended lesson, but instead observes to see what the child really did learn. An easy smile and gentle encouragement help the child to proceed confidently, at her own speed.

Teachers can make it convenient for children to teach each other, the very best reinforcement of learning.

All learning is sequential; children take each step with pleasure if it is carefully introduced. Dr. George Crane points out that "the motion brings on the emotion," and children get interested in the things they are used to.

A child needs freedom to create what *he* wants to create without anyone's asking "What is it?" The best reply came from a three-year-old boy who answered his scientist father, "Why, it's paint on paper, Daddy, what did you think?"

The most helpful teachers appreciate creative accomplishment, but do not question or correct it unless invited to do so by the creator. These boys have been building airplanes and helicopters under the supervision of the school custodian, who regularly does carpentry with them. The boys are delighted with their lop-sided creations; the custodian's comment was neither a criticism nor a suggestion, but the observation that they "handle the saw and hammer better each time." When children are ready, they will ask questions about improving their work.

As children begin to build structures with a purpose, rather than simply to manipulate blocks, they like to join in group efforts. In this school all the children are given turns to discuss their work. With teacher guidance, the group volunteers information or asks questions. For example, there may be a discussion of how the car will get into the upper level of the parking garage without a ramp. Some schools photograph the children's work; in this school, the teacher makes a sketch of the child's block structure that he can take home.

Simple materials can provide lessons in action and result, cause and effect. Food preparation shows immediate results. Also, children can toss pebbles into water to watch the ripples, or drop leaves into a stream to see which way it's flowing. Machines are endlessly instructive: pushing typewriter keys, pouring water through a funnel into tubes, whirling washers on a metal screw rod, working pulleys.

This school has experimented successfully with tape recorders and other machines that allow each child to learn at his own speed. At the large round table, the boys are listening to the tape of a fairy tale recorded by their teacher. In the foreground, one boy is practicing typing on an electric typewriter. The other is working on a programmed phonics lesson. Not all schools have access to such a variety of machines, but many encourage a parent with a tape recorder to do volunteer work with individuals or very small groups. Children are fascinated by the sound of their own voices, and recording helps them to develop verbal skills.

Lower case letters are used in this classroom when children are ready for alphabet games. This is of the utmost importance since books are printed in lower case.

White chalk boards and dark chalk help children transfer their learning to white paper and dark print. The chalk boards are made of unfinished formica, or of heavily painted masonite, and they wipe clean with tissue.

Large print makes reading easier. A child is encouraged to learn the symbols for his name, address, and telephone number, and to put his name on his work when he is able.

A child's name identifies all his accomplishments. Here, it is printed around the hole he drills, and each takes home his circlet of wood.

Rapid learners like to go on to special projects with individual guidance. This girl is making an alphabet book. Some pages are decorated with her own drawings, some with pictures clipped from magazines, some with little collages: a piece of straw on the "S" page, for instance, or yarn on the "Y" page.

An "interest book" is a record of individual projects. This child's photograph and the things she has studied are assembled here. Her school encourages an interest in science and her family will probably learn a lot when she takes her booklet home. Children's interests may range from butterflies to dentistry. The important thing is that they make the choice and do the work themselves.

Games like "postal clerk" help children learn to read their friends' names.

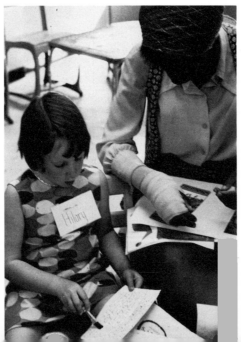

Children are proud to be asked to make something "for the school." This teacher starts them out doing individual abstract designs on tiny pieces of driftwood to take home. They use white glue, pebbles, pine needles, anything from a nature walk. Later, she encourages them to cooperate on a large three-dimensional project. The teacher is careful to see that each child who works on the big project also has something to take home that day, to ease his feelings about leaving a part of himself at school.

Children delight in helping keep their school in repair. Any child may want to oil the wheel equipment once; those who are really interested will pursue it and understand *why* they are doing it.

Children take pleasure in their own maintenance and clean-up: straightening a rug, waxing the slide by sitting on waxed paper,

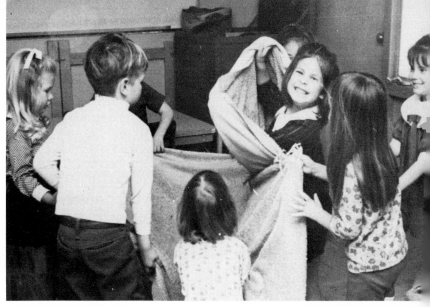

spreading window cleaner, and wiping it off, with a child on each side of the glass,

sifting and cleaning the sand. The children and the "grandfather aide" built the sifter from an old wooden box and some screen. The boy in the background is waterbrushing the fence. Children like to "paint" the equipment with water—it makes everything look a bit shinier (and in fact does clean it).

Some teachers sing a "clean-up song" or give a musical cue about fifteen minutes before closing, so that children have time to wind up activities and to participate happily in jobs they enjoy.

Cleaning up helps to channel energies into useful outlets.

Music ends the day pleasantly, and children can leave more easily in the middle of a song than in the middle of a story.

Teachers give their all each day, even though they know they should try to save energy for essential evaluations and planning after pupils have left and clean-up is completed.

THE ENVIRONMENT

The effectiveness of a school is determined by the atmosphere that prevails, not by the building in which the school is housed. Children may flourish in a handsome setting like this old mansion, now the University of Southern California Preschool,

but they may do just as well in a commercial district—an environment which children find fascinating. This school is located under a freeway overpass.

Each child needs about a hundred square feet of yard space. The open-vented fence is non-splintery. There are both sunny and shady areas.

This sturdy, imaginative fence doubles as a spot for privacy and shade in an otherwise large, open yard.

A covered area outdoors is good for storage and for play in bad weather.

Balancing is a natural instinct in children. This skill relates to their physical readiness for concentrating and controlling body movements—hence their ability to read and write. Balance boards are easy projects for a group of children to make with the aid of a carpentry-minded adult.

Safety is a prime consideration in outdoor equipment. Corners are rounded and moving parts or bolts checked regularly. These children are edging table corners with strips from old motorcycle tires.

Raw materials are better than most commercial toys in outdoor play areas. Hinged planks and saw horses are in use here.

Children need free space to run in. Yard equipment may be rotated often or stored so that some play area remains uncluttered.

Not all outdoor equipment is bulky. Easily maneuverable items are good for imaginative games and are not a great storage problem. Children like to pump the inner tubes daily.

A discarded hose can be a gas pump.

A supply of basic items like boards, springs, ropes, and tires allows a child to build what he wants.

Easels and work tables can be set outdoors whenever possible.

This sturdy climbing rope is kept looped out of reach unless an adult is nearby, and children who learn to climb it have a resonant reward.

These sand containers are made of galvanized cans. The boys and girls sweep the spilled sand into the dust pan at the end of the day and re-fill the cans. The sand is usually kept damp for molding purposes. When it rains, a garbage can cover fits snugly.

Water play areas allow for the pleasures of slush, gush, and mud. Indoor water tables are another possibility, if space permits. (The surrounding floor can be protected with sheets of plastic.) In good weather, some schools take groups of children to a safe lakeside.

A well-tended climbing tree can double as a story-telling spot.

A wide slide encourages cooperation instead of competition.

After children have mastered a basic skill, they enjoy an added challenge. She feels that she is parachuting.

Children love crawlers and other happy hiding places. These pipes were donated by a nearby road crew because of slight cracks in their bases. Mothers painted and decorated them.

Sturdy equipment like this can be used by one child or several at a time. Because these items are abstract in design, they lend themselves to creative play. They can be cars, horses, boats, airplanes, castles, magic carpets.

It's fun to have one absolutely unique thing to play with. This old boat was donated to the school and sits on the lawn, rain or shine. The children are building a "dock" in the background. They like to sail toward the dock, pretend the grass is water, and save each other from the ocean. This boat is never anything but a boat, but it provides hours of constructive play.

Rigging ropes are great for climbing, and children love the combination of climb and sway. It took everyone in the school about two months to make this rigging. The largest, heaviest ropes are separated into strands by a teacher using an awl, while a child works the next size rope through. The ends are difficult; strands of each rope are separated and then woven together. Sometimes the ends are also bound with electrician's tape. The rigging can be hung on an old metal swing frame, or on trees, or on a scaffolding built for it. The final hanging is extremely bulky and heavy. A good strong crew accomplishes it while the children cheer.

Many schools refuse to have swings. Staff must be right on the spot to supervise their use, and most children have already experienced swings either at home or in parks. Schools that feel swings are worthwhile should choose them thoughtfully and avoid the usual kind with open seats, tippy boards, splinters, square corners, and chains. With this swing a teacher must help the child in and out. The circle of wood gives the child a secure feeling, and she cannot possibly slip out. Waxy ropes are sturdy and smooth. When the swings are not in use, they are hung out of reach. In this school, the swings hang from a ceiling beam in the outdoor covered area. Children can swing either from covered area to open area, or entirely under cover on rainy days.

Both outdoor and indoor areas need empty spaces between activity centers, where a child may watch from a comfortable distance while deciding when to become involved.

Creative schools are lively places. The most ordinary materials can be used imaginatively to produce an interesting environment and a climate of learning.

Some families who form small cooperative schools take turns meeting at each member's approved home. The children enjoy the variety.

Some kind of locker or cubbyhole is essential as a gathering place for each child's art work, damp pants, rain hat, lunch box, or show and tell item. There are many possible locker designs. The simplest are clusters of cylindrical half-gallon ice cream cartons bound together to form pigeonholes. Some schools use shoe boxes on shelves, or commercial plastic vegetable bins. The important thing is that the locker belongs to the child and bears his name. Everything else in the school may be community property, but the locker is a sacred and personal place.

Many nursery schools are housed in older buildings that are not readily convertible to large open classrooms. But tops of walls can be cut out and peeking places can be created between rooms. Children like to check up on what is happening all around them; a sort of learning-by-osmosis occurs. Peeking places are good spots for children who may watch a particular activity for a long time—perhaps months—before trying it.

All bulletin boards are child height except the one used by parents or teachers.

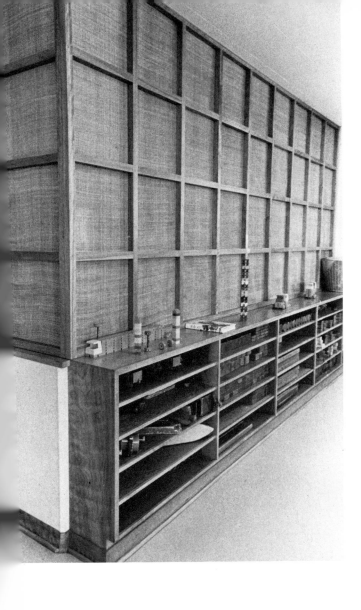

Community schools like to encourage visitors and try to have a place where they can be made welcome without distracting staff and pupils. This is the schoolroom side of an observation "wall" created by a grass cloth screen. Visitors can watch and listen unnoticed from the other side. Materials are kept on hand to answer observers' questions, so that teachers need not talk about the class in front of the children. Visiting hours are considerately controlled. After all, the purpose of a school is to serve its students, and visitors come second.

Toilets may be installed at a height that is handy for each age group. This splendid bathroom in a large new school has doors that open both to the yard and to the classrooms. More modest schools need not despair. When most schools open, particularly in old buildings, they need more toilets to meet the building code requirements. Wall-mounted toilets can be set at child level, even if the budget requires second-hand appliances.

Parents may relax about toilet training because socializing at school will solve that problem for any healthy child. Most nursery schools have no partitions in bathrooms for practical reasons—access is quicker and fingers don't get pinched in doors. Very nice, natural sex education takes place as it would in a large family. Some kindergartens continue this "open door" policy, others start teaching reading by labeling doors "boys" and "girls."

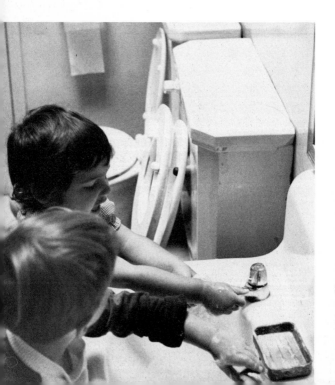

When a school has a day care program, privacy is a special consideration. These children take naps on cots separated by screens, so that each has his own private place. The screens become personal bulletin boards decorated with scissor cut-outs, leaves, paper dolls, art work, hair bows, snake skins—whatever pleases the child.

Children may return to napping when they start school, because of the stimulation of group activities. At school as at home, a child's daily energy, moods, and metabolism are also affected by changes in weather, winds, and barometric pressure.

Easily accessible book shelves invite children to read in every room. They like to carry a book to a table or favorite chair.

Open shelving lets the children keep equipment neatly organized (and supplementary storage areas ensure that equipment can be rotated).

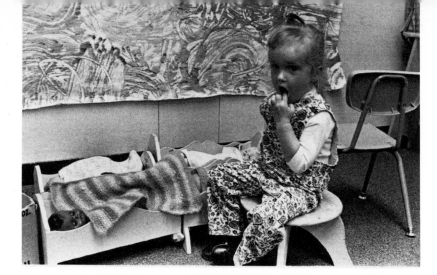

Every child needs times of repose and places to relax and be quiet within herself.

In this school each block is outlined at the back of the shelf, and teams of "lumbermen" are responsible for keeping the blocks in the building areas.

This is a "house corner" where children play house and where real teaching about real things can take place. The child-size appliances are sturdily made of wood or molded plastic. They do not work, but the counter tops are big enough to prepare things on. The children then take their food to the big kitchen if it needs to be cooked. (Many recipes do not.) A pan of soapy water can be set in the play sink and real dishes can be washed.

There is a large mirror in the house corner where children can study themselves at various stages in their growth—or in various identities. He is dressing up as a Cub Scout. Clean, fresh, attractive dress-up clothes can be rotated often. Girls have no trouble assembling costumes; small boys like to wear animal costumes and official hats, or suits, shoes, and bow ties donated by ten-year-olds.

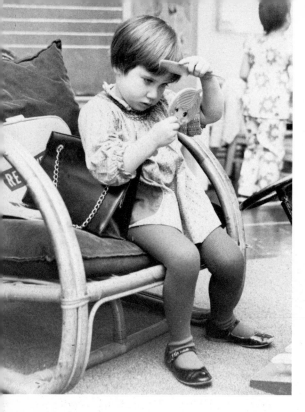

Some activities are most attractive to girls

and some are open to all comers.

Health-conscious teachers sterilize the earplugs of stethoscopes between uses. Other things that should be sterilized or discarded: tongue depressors brought by a dentist's assistant who shows children dental molds of baby teeth and demonstrates how to brush them. Dental instruments brought to allay fears. Police whistles. Musical instruments (except harmonicas, which are impossible to clean).

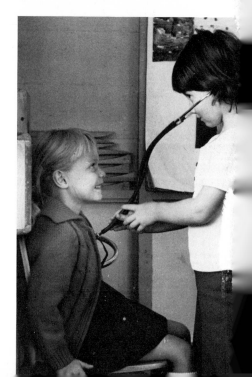

Real telephones are good for make-believe conversations. (Some children won't talk to people, but will talk to a phone!) The telephone company is usually glad to donate old unwired phones. The dials work and the teacher can give lessons in answering the phone, or in making a phone call.

Workbenches and real tools encourage eye–hand coordination. In this school, tables are covered with rubber matting or a carpet end so the wood does not slip and noise is lessened. (Large nails can be pushed through corks or bottle tops for easy handling.) The small hammers have rubber grip handles and seven-to thirteen-ounce heads.

not many schools use them because they are too much trouble; only a few children can use the workbench at a time, and they need diplomatic supervision by someone who knows what he or she is doing. A good solution is to find a carpentry-minded volunteer or "grandfather aide."

Children enjoy making music with real instruments, scaled to nursery–kindergarten size. They are expensive but well-constructed and durable. They fit small hands and are more encouraging for beginners than full-size instruments. Home-made instruments are just as much fun; children like to make them from frozen orange juice cans, broomsticks, sandpaper, wooden blocks, and bells.

Children should be given man-sized tools. Toy tools are so flimsy that they break when used correctly, and only frustrate the child. A three-year-old can use the smallest adult screwdriver quite well. Unfortunately, not many children work with tools at home, and

Equipment can be both attractive and easily accessible to the child—for instance, magnetic or flannel boards with abstract and specific accessories.

These children are testing an experimental flannel board cut diagonally from a carton, one surface covered with felt. One school makes *all* its flannel boards and easels from boxes; it can then store enough for each child in the same space that would be required to store one regular easel.

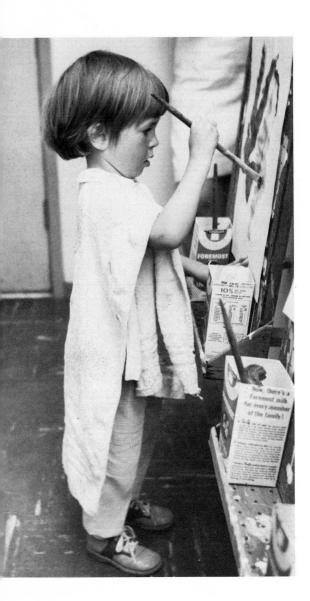

All equipment is selected to encourage independence. These easels and self-donning smocks enable a child to paint without calling for a teacher. The pegboard easels hang on the wall indoors or on the fence outdoors, and the child pegs the paper. They are also used on tables as low-slant easels for inky substances or as pegboards with colorful golf tees. Mothers donate towels with slits in the center for smocks.

A school can never have too many abstract, non-directive toys. Here, colorful rubber bands and another kind of pegboard.

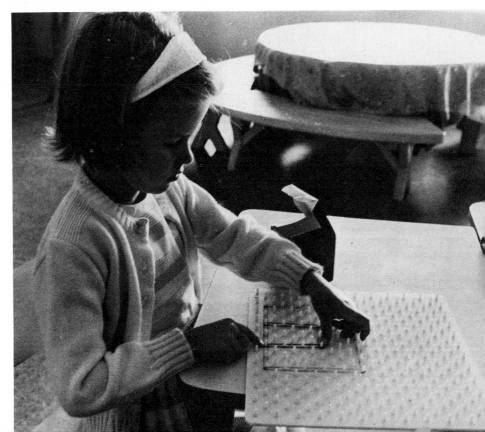

Large colorful cloth swatches and indoor boxes or blocks lend themselves to creative play.

Children first master achievement-level puzzles, then go on to create their own games with the puzzle pieces. Toddlers start with simple three-piece puzzles; older children, or very mechanically-minded ones, can do puzzles of twenty-five or thirty pieces. Knob puzzles develop the finger dexterity needed later for handwriting.

Versatile toys are a blessing because of storage and budget problems. This one is, first of all, an excellent puzzle. While fitting the right piece into the right hole, the child learns to identify shapes and colors. Numbers on the piece correspond to the number of sides on the piece, and there are dots for counting the numbers. If the child is very advanced, the teacher sets the timer to see if he can complete the puzzle in, say, one minute. (Preschoolers can do this puzzle in as little as fourteen seconds. Adults often take as long as thirty seconds.) This puzzle makes a nice rhythm instrument, too. The pieces are also useful at the craft table for cutting play dough or for dipping in thick tempera to make geometric designs on construction paper.

Abstract concepts can be given concrete meaning with visual and tactile aids. Cuissenaire rods and large floor rods help new learners quickly comprehend the number bases. After this orderly introduction, children need free space and time to experiment with the subject by themselves.

A well-planned room offers many opportunities for number and reading games.

Gravity is a concept which some thoughtful children never quite accept. "Why should everything go down when birds and rockets go up?"

The trucks are going down a ramp sturdy enough for a child to slide down. Any gravity or pulley toy fascinates children because it is something the child starts and the toy carries on involuntarily. Many cautious children will never use a slide or whirly-go-round or anything that makes them lose control. This kind of child often gets extra pleasure from a toy that does the out-of-control thing for him.

Machines, both simple and complicated, interest children in letters, arts, and sciences. There is a plastic window in the side of this typewriter.

An electrician father helped the children build this battery board. Each wire does something: one rings a bell, one lights a light, one makes a propeller spin when the circuit is completed.

A teacher constructed this scale for the children in her snack group, and they give out raisins, crackers, pea pods, or whatever, according to weight. Each child takes delight in getting exactly as much food as the others; fussy eaters are drawn into the game; greedy ones would rather be accurate than greedy.

Sound containers like these can be bought, but they are easy to make at home from identical painted metal bandage boxes. They are filled with objects that make a variety of noises, from soft to loud, when the box is shaken. The game is to arrange the sealed boxes according to volume. The contents might be tea leaves, sand, cloth buttons, pins, nails, rocks, in order of noisiness.

Aquariums, terrariums, and ant farms are valuable and easy to maintain. In this school the children also make a "bug house" by cutting out one side of a milk carton and inserting it into an old nylon stocking. Each day there is a "bug ceremony" to free insects captured that day. When they observe insects, children feel big in comparison; they learn respect both for the balance of nature and for useful bugs.

Grass is fun, too. Children can plant seeds in egg crates or terrariums and cut the grass with scissors. Terrariums can be filled with local flora found in the yard or on a nature walk.

At the science table, pupils expect to find a different aspect of the sciences every week or so. This zoologist mother brought in a cat skull which she found in a vacant lot. Science tables are most effective if they are limited to one subject at a time. An excellent starting subject is the child's own body. A physiology table offers a small plastic skeleton, anatomy book, stethoscope, mirrors, and a chart of eye colors. Children study their own eyes and put their names under the proper color on the chart. A tooth chart, with a regular mirror and dental mirror, is awe-inspiring.

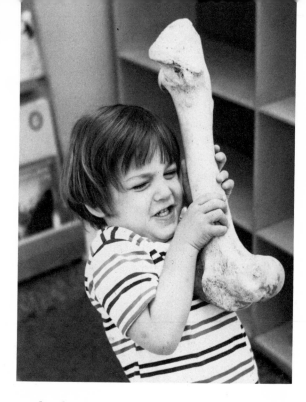

This boy is holding a cow's femur, which his teacher found while hiking and brought in for an impromptu lesson. It led to much discussion. The children raised questions like what would happen to you if you didn't have bones? Why are some bones small and some bones large? How do bones bend? Why are different bones different shapes? Do bones grow? Do all animals have bones?

Magnifying glasses and microscopes can be used both indoors and outdoors, on things from the science table or on everyday objects in the classroom or parts of the child's own body. After children get used to magnifying glasses, a leaf never again looks as abstract to them as it did. A bug is not a blob again, but a creature with wings and a pulse. We are so jaded by so many stimuli that our children, if they follow our daily example, glance but do not *see*. The concentration of using a microscope to study, say, a page of print, to see that it consists of many dots, enlarges a child's concept of matter as much as it momentarily enlarges his sight. One child expressed it this way: "I found my way into a new place where my feet can't go, only my head."

Most nursery equipment is for big muscle strengthening, but small muscle coordination is equally important. Poker chips are difficult to pick up but little fingers can do it and there is a satisfying sense of accomplishment. Children like to stack them, sort them by color, roll them on the table, build with them. Items like this, brought from home, provide variety. Another advantage is that these items may be forbidden at home—many things are—and a child is pleased to have an opportunity to use something Mother won't let her use. It takes the lure out of the forbidden.

Parents can contribute scraps of otherwise waste materials to the school for abstract creative purposes: decorative paper ends, plastic packing, egg cartons, wood and metal bits and pieces,

old boxes, wheels, and broom handles, for children to construct—
in this case, a train. Part of the child's pleasure in building is in
choosing his own materials.

Broken clocks, typewriters, or small appliances are interesting
to disassemble. Perhaps parents can also donate a half hour of
their time to help the children get started. Parents who work on
projects with their children at home, too, help them feel that the
joy of learning does not end when they leave school.

It is an eye-opener for parents to do volunteer work with special children: physically crippled or emotionally disturbed or developmentally different or gifted learners. All teachers in training must work with or observe special children. If a parent too can know the immense range of learning patterns, he can see his own child with wiser perspective.

A school can be an "extended family" that offers daily encouragement and is on hand in times of crisis. Good teachers take time to care and to listen; problems that seem impossible to parents often

Families enrich the life of the school by sharing special foods or customs. This family has brought a Japanese tea party, including the screen designed by a family member.

Many schools invite younger brothers and sisters to come for a short visit. Making the parent feel at home in the school is a sure sign of a caring staff. Considerate parents cooperate in mutual support of the school.

assume more reasonable proportions when shared with an experienced and sensible teacher.

The greatest gift a school or a parent can give a child is to acknowledge his uniqueness and offer loving encouragement to his special ways.

DEVELOPING SKILLS

Nursery and kindergarten teachers have always considered it important to encourage compatibility, creativity, knowledge of the environment, and inductive reasoning. Along with these they try to help each child develop some skills. Even when a child is fearfully timid or overtly aggressive, he may be aided by the confidence that a useful skill can induce.

In a public school yard-duty program, a fighting six-year-old came to me in tears of fury. He was being ridiculed by the other children because he could not blow bubble gum. It seemed that Mike's single parent had forbidden gum at home and no friend had ever shown him how. After a half hour of instruction on where to hold his tongue, how to suck the air, and how to blow controlled air by holding his nose at first, Mike learned the invaluable lesson that skill can be achieved through practice and by following directions. He soon blew the most impressive bubbles. As he began trying to learn things instead of "knowing it all," children stopped teasing "monster Mike who can't do anything." He became a new child on the schoolground.

A child exhibiting behavior extremes such as Mike's belligerence has had his confidence damaged in some way. While penny bubble gum mastery is not exactly studied in Education courses, the incident dramatized for me the expedient of patching a child's punctured confidence by encouraging a simple skill.

Another type of situation arose when a delicate five-year-old girl, Sue, was unable to cut paper. Her frailness and her ambidextrous tendencies confused her scissors skill and impaired other motor abilities—and possibly her brain patterns, for Sue was not academically talented either. She loved to make things out of paper, however, and kept trying to succeed at the craft table. After a conference at school, her father had the brilliant idea of taking her to a hardware store where he persisted until they found a fine, perfectly balanced pair of scissors that she could handle. She learned to cut, and created attractive craft projects with her own scissors. Throughout Sue's years of school life, she artistically rounded the four corners of every homework or notebook assignment and also developed a nice round handwriting, which made her papers a pleasure to read.

Another unforgettable little boy, Tony, could not afford to buy me a flower, nor did he have flowers growing in his apartment area as did some classmates. He feared picking one because his strict parents had over-lectured him on theft. One day while others were presenting attractive posies, he shyly gave me a dirt-caked seed he'd found near a bush. We planted the seed in a paper cup and by some magic providence the dried-up thing finally sprouted. The class had sweet potato vines around the room and Tony told me he prayed nightly that his plant would be as green and beautiful as the vines. (Note that he had given it to me, but as it grew it became his again.) We moved it from cup to can to pot as it enlarged. Instead of being a compact bush, it seemed leggy like a sick fern. At last we set the scrawny thing in a boggy corner of the yard and it took off like Jack's beanstalk. To condense a long story, it became a giant acacia tree, the landmark of the school, and Tony became a botany teacher.

The skills we help develop in young children may seem simple, but they are important and they grow. We adults must realize how precious a child's accomplishment is to him. A picture, a tune, a block structure, a leaf he wants to show—we should respect him and his skills just as we wish that he learn respect for himself, others, and the world around him.

tying

skipping

blowing controlled air

folding and stapling

cutting

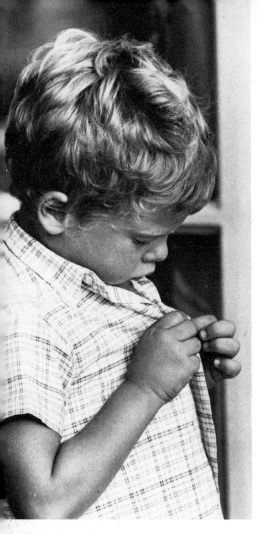

buttoning

pouring

whistling

climbing

gluing

singing

punching holes

hammering

jumping

coordinating jumps and claps

gripping

The Photographers

ROBERT OVERSTREET

There is no keener student of the young than Robert Overstreet. For twenty-six years he has spent full time recording the action in nursery schools. "Overstreet Day" at schools in Northern California is a very special time for staffs and parents because they know they will get some views of their children that even they had not seen before.

To the thousands who have observed his modus operandi it will come as no surprise that his insight, love, and respect for children show in his enlightening photographs.

His pictures are used in textbooks, magazines, newspapers, and brochures. He is so adept at camera work that he often "shoots from the hip" while children are unaware of his intent.

He has had the experience of raising seven of his own, and the background of the psychology books by his father, the late Harry Overstreet. His degree was taken in Sociology at the University of Chicago.

Robert Overstreet has quietly carried the word on equipment and creative ideas from one school to another; now through his participation in this book, the sharing can be on a wider scale.

MICHELLE VIGNES

Originally from France, Michelle Vignes has been photographing in the United States since 1965. Her work appears regularly in leading magazines here and in Europe.

For several years before free-lancing, she was a picture editor for Magnum Photos and for the United Nations Educational, Scientific and Cultural Organization in Paris.

Her poignant style was heightened by her work with world-renowned photographer Henri Cartier-Bresson. Following a formal education in France, she has continued to study psychology and philosophy.

Her assignments are often with emotionally involving subjects that require "soul" or a delicate blend of subjectivity and objectivity. She specializes in photographic essays and her sensitivity and skill show in such tender themes as a Symanon marathon encounter. When time permits, she does portrait studies.

Over the years, Miss Vignes has found great appeal in American children's independence and initiative. She seeks those unique expressions inherent in young personalities, and her pictures capture relationships and moods as well as they can be imprinted on paper.

"ALISSA"

Alissa is typical of today's enterprising youth, only to the extent that she has so many interests. Two of her energy outlets are working with young children and doing professional photography. She does both paid and volunteer aide work in nursery schools, and is presently a senior in photography at California State University. Her effortless approach to taking pictures belies the work she has done in building her own darkroom and studying the chemistry of developing. Her award-winning pictures appear in exhibits, newspapers, trade publications, and *Friends Journal*, which first published her. With her engineer father and family she has lived or travelled in every state except Florida and Alaska. Imbued with today's teen spirit, she hopes her efforts can eventually help bring the country into better focus.

OTHER PHOTOGRAPHERS:

1. *John Fell Stevenson*'s photographic talents include his knack of developing prints with a three-dimensional essence. He did the photographic record of his late father, Adlai Stevenson, United Nations Ambassador.

2. *Barbara Miles* and her family have always worked with and for American Indian groups in the Southern California–Arizona border areas. She is one of the few who can approach any of their various modes of life with a camera.

3. *Iolani School Audio-Visual Department.*

KEY: Page number, Left, Right, Center, Top, Bottom

OVERSTREET: 21L, 23L, 25R, 26, 27R, 28C, 29, 30L, 32, 34, 35, 36L, 37R, 46L&B, 47, 48, 50L, 52L, 54R, 55, 56, 58R, 59, 60R, 66L, 67R, 69R, 70TL, 71, 72TR, 73R, 75T, 78R, 79L&B, 80TR, 82, 83R, 84L, 85, 87R, 88L, 90, 93TR, 95, 96L&TR, 97R, 98, 99L, 100L, 101R, 102, 103R, 104, 105, 106, 107, 110L, 111, 118L, 121L, 122, 123R

VIGNES: 23C, 24, 25L, 27L, 28L&R, 31R, 33L, 36R, 37L; 38, 39, 40R, 45TL&TR, 49, 50R, 51BR, 52R, 57L, 60L, 61, 63L, 64L&BR, 65, 66BR, 67L, 68R, 69BL, 70BR, 74, 78L, 83L, 86TL, 88TR&BR, 89, 91, 92BR, 93BR, 94TR, 97L, 99R, 100R, 101BL&TC, 103L, 108, 109, 115L&TR, 118R, 120L&C, 121R, 123L

"ALISSA": 21R, 22, 31L, 33R, 41, 42, 43, 44, 45B, 46TR, 51T, 53, 54L, 57R, 58L, 62, 63R, 64T, 69TL, 70BC, 72L&BR, 73L, 75BR, 76, 79TR, 80L&BR, 81, 84R, 86R&BL, 87L, 92L&TR, 94L&B, 96BR, 110R, 112, 113, 114, 115BR, 117, 119, 120R, 121C

STEVENSON: 23R, 77

MILES: 30R

IOLANI: 40L, 68L, 93TL

Nursery and Kindergarten Associations

Associations sponsor workshops, meetings, or conferences to serve the needs of teachers, administrators, and interested parents. Some gatherings are limited to a few dozen persons registered in advance. Other conventions handle thousands and bring world-wide experts, speakers, and exhibitors together. For information on branches, contact these central offices:

American Montessori Society
175 Fifth Avenue
New York, N.Y. 10010

American Association of Elementary–Kindergarten–Nursery Educators, National Education Association Center
1201 Sixteenth Street, N.W.
Washington, D.C. 20036

Association for Childhood Education International
3615 Wisconsin Avenue, N.W.
Washington, D.C. 20016

National Association for the Education of Young Children
1834 Connecticut Avenue, N.W.
Washington, D.C. 20009

Parent Cooperative Preschools International
20551 Lakeshore Road
Baie d'Urfe 850
Quebec, Canada

Local public school offices can give information concerning groups meeting regularly in their areas. Private nursery schools can provide data on other local associations. These associations, as well as local licensing agencies, act as clearing houses for information on starting and maintaining good schools.

Bibliography

BOOKS

Boone, J. Allen. *Kinship With All Life*. New York: Harper & Row, 1954. An adult male exemplifies the same attitude toward animal life that very young children seem to have but cannot express.

Bowlby, John. *Child Care and the Growth of Love*. New York: Pelican Books, 1959. A classic on attitudes toward childhood.

Bremer, Anne and John. *Open Education*. New York: Holt, Rinehart & Winston, 1972. A combination of the best of old education's wisdom and the new freedom.

Carabo-Cone, Madeleine, and Royt, Beatrice. *How To Help Children Learn Music*. New York: Harper & Row, 1953. Delightful ways to learn together.

Edwards, Dr. Esther. *Wonder of Growing*. Chicago: Sears, Roebuck & Company, 1973. A fine guide for the years from birth through pre-school.

Encyclopaedia Britannica. *Pre-School Library*. Chicago, 1972. Adventures in the basics—clocks, numbers, colors, language, etc., in 13 small volumes.

Ginott, Haim G. *Between Parent and Child*. New York: The Macmillan Company, 1965. Establishing wholesome patterns of communication.

Hewes, Dorothy, and Hartman, Barbara. *Early Childhood Education: A Workbench for Administrators*. San Francisco: R and E Research Associates, 1972. A practical guide for becoming involved in a school.

Hollander, Cornelia H. *Portable Workshop for Pre-School Teachers*. New York: Doubleday & Company, Inc., 1966. Specific curriculum to use as points of departure.

Holt, John. *How Children Learn*. New York: Pitman Publishing Corporation, 1967. Straightforward examples of learning situations.

Homan, William E. *Child Sense*. New York: Basic Books, 1969. A pediatrician's sensible suggestions.

Hopkins, Lee Bennett. *Children's Literature—A Balanced Collection for Teachers*. New York: Citation Press, 1971. 2 professional books for staff; 15 award-winning children's books; and a teaching guide.

Hymes, James L., Jr. *Teaching the Child Under Six*. Columbus, Ohio: Merrill Publishing Company, 1968. Informative, comprehensive classic.

Kellogg, Rhoda. *Analyzing Children's Art*. Palo Alto: National Book Press, 1969. After this book every scribble a child makes is appreciated.

Miller, Mabel Evelyn. *A Practical Guide for Kindergarten Teachers*. West Nyack, New York: Parker Publishing Company, 1970. For staff, by an experienced classroom teacher. Nothing "theoretical."

Prudden, Suzy, and Sussman, Jeffrey. *Creative Fitness for Baby and Child*. New York: William Morrow & Company, 1972. Encourages parents to play physically with young children.

Rambusch, Nancy McCormick. *Learning How To Learn*. New York: Garmand Press, 1962. An American approach to Montessori.

Sharp, Evelyn. *Thinking Is Child's Play*. New York: E. P. Dutton & Company, 1969. Piaget research translated into fun for schools.

Southern California Association for Education of Young Children. *Administration of Schools for Young Children*. Pasadena, 1972. More help for school personnel.

Taylor, Katharine Whiteside. *Parents and Children Learn Together*. Columbia University: Teachers College Press, 1968. The "bible" for anyone starting a school or becoming a "cooperating parent."

Todd, Vivian, and Heffernan, Helen. *The Years Before School*. New York: The Macmillan Company, 1970. Excellent road map to ages 2 to 6, from swimming to "thinking."

MAGAZINES AND PAMPHLETS

"Alabama Guide for Kindergarten Teachers." State Department of Education, Montgomery, Alabama 36104. Booklet.

"Children." Office of Child Development, U.S. Department of Health, Education, and Welfare, Washington, D.C. 20201. Magazine.

"Discipline in the Nursery School." Golden Gate Kindergarten Association, 1315 Ellis Street, San Francisco, California 94115. Pamphlet.

"Don't Push Me!" Association for Childhood Education International, 3615 Wisconsin Avenue, N.W., Washington, D.C. 20016. Pamphlet.

"Formative Years." Country Day School, Westway 34, Fairfield, Iowa 52556. Bulletin.

"Housing for Early Childhood Education." Association for Childhood Education International, 3615 Wisconsin Avenue, N.W., Washington, D.C. 20016. Booklet.

"New Schools Manual." New Directions Community School, 445 Tenth Street, Richmond, California 94801. Manual on tax forms needed to start a school.

"Nursery School Portfolio." Association for Childhood Education International, 3615 Wisconsin Avenue, N.W., Washington, D.C. 20016. Leaflets on starting and operating a school.

"Parent Cooperative Newsletter." Whiteside Taylor Centre for Cooperative Education, 20551 Lakeshore Road, Baie d'Urfe 850, Quebec, Canada. Bulletin.

"Parents' Guide to the Montessori Classroom." Penn-Mont Academy, 2733 Sixth Avenue, Altoona, Pennsylvania 16602. Leaflets.

"Ready or Not." Research Concepts, 1368 East Airport Road, Muskegon, Michigan 49444. Pamphlet.

"Today's Child." Edwards Publications, Inc., 92A Nassau Street, Princeton, New Jersey 08540. Newsletter.

"Workjobs." Addison-Wesley, Menlo Park, California, or Reading, Massachusetts, London or Ontario. Booklet.